Giftbooks in this "Words for Life" series:

Words on Hope Words on Joy
Words on Courage Words on Kindness
Words of Wisdom Words on Love and Caring
Words on Compassion Words on Solitude and Silence
Words on Beauty Words on Strength and Perseverance
Words on Calm Words on a Simple Life

Published simultaneously in 1998 by Exley Publications Ltd. in
Great Britain, and Exley Publications LLC in the USA.
Copyright © Helen Exley 1998
The moral right of the author has been asserted.

12 11 10 9 8 7 6 5 4 3 2

Edited and pictures selected by Helen Exley
ISBN 1-86187-056-6

Picture research by Image Select International
Printed in China.

**Exley Publications Ltd, 16 Chalk Hill, Watford,
Herts WD1 4BN, UK.
Exley Publications LLC, 232 Madison Avenue,
Suite 1206, NY 10016, USA.**

Words on Calm

A HELEN EXLEY GIFTBOOK

EXLEY

NEW YORK • WATFORD, UK

THE MIRACLE COMES
QUIETLY INTO THE
MIND THAT STOPS AN
INSTANT AND IS STILL

FROM
"A COURSE IN MIRACLES"

Contentment... comes as the infallible result of great acceptances, great humilities – of not trying to make ourselves this or that (to conform to some dramatized version of ourselves), but of surrendering ourselves to the fullness of life – of letting life flow through us.

DAVID GRAYSON

*W*hy should we live with such hurry and waste of life? ... Men say that a stitch in time saves nine, and so they take a thousand stitches today to save nine tomorrow. As for work, we haven't any of any consequence. We have Saint Vitus' dance, and cannot possibly keep our heads still.

HENRY DAVID THOREAU
(1817-1862)

*L*isten in deep silence.
Be very still and open
your mind....
Sink deep into the
peace that waits for you
beyond the frantic,
riotous thoughts and
sights and sounds of
this insane world.

FROM "A COURSE IN MIRACLES"

*S*erenity is neither
frivolity, nor
complacency, it is the
highest knowledge
and love, it is the
affirmation of all
reality being awake
at the edge of all
deeps and abysses.
Serenity is the secret
of beauty and the real
substance of all art.

HERMANN HESSE (1877-1962)

THE SERENE HAVE
NOT OPTED OUT OF LIFE.
THEY SEE MORE
WIDELY, LOVE MORE
DEARLY, REJOICE IN
THE THINGS THE
FRANTIC MIND NO
LONGER SEES OR
HEARS.

PAM BROWN, b.1928

Leave home in the sunshine:
Dance through a meadow –
Or sit by a stream and just be.
The lilt of the water
Will gather your worries
And carry them down to the sea.

J. DONALD WALTERS

*S*erenity does not
cancel hope or
adventure,
work or love.
It flows through the
landscape of our
busy lives,
quiet and strong.
Clear and gentle.
Refreshing all we do
or dream.

PAM BROWN, b.1928

Work is not always *required of a man. There is such a thing as sacred idleness, the cultivation of which is now fearfully neglected.*

GEORGE MACDONALD (1824-1905)

IF YOU CAN SPEND A PERFECTLY USELESS AFTERNOON IN A PERFECTLY USELESS MANNER, YOU HAVE LEARNED HOW TO LIVE.

LIN YUTANG (1895-1976)

*P*eace is the
fairest form of
happiness.

WILLIAM ELLERY CHANNING
(1780–1842)

Teach me the art of
creating islands of
stillness, in which I
can absorb the
beauty of everyday
things: clouds, trees,
a snatch of music....

MARION STROUD

DON'T HURRY DON'T WORRY, YOU'RE ONLY HERE FOR A SHORT VISIT. SO BE SURE TO STOP AND SMELL THE FLOWERS

WALTER HAGAN

Whatever peace I know rests in the natural world, in feeling myself a part of it, even in a small way.

MAY SARTON,
FROM "JOURNAL OF A SOLITUDE"

*OUR GREATEST
EXPERIENCES ARE
OUR QUIETEST
MOMENTS.*

NIETZSCHE (1844-1900)

Happiness is as a butterfly, which, when pursued, is always beyond our grasp, but which, if you will sit down quietly, may alight upon you.

NATHANIEL HAWTHORNE (1804-1864)

The way to use life is to do nothing through acting, The way to use life is to do everything through being.

LAO-TZU

Do not let trifles disturb your tranquillity of mind.... Life is too precious to be sacrificed for the nonessential and transient.... Ignore the inconsequential.

GRENVILLE KLEISER

There is, perhaps, no solitary sensation so exquisite as that of slumbering on the grass or hay, shaded from the hot sun by a tree, with the consciousness of a fresh light air running through the wide atmosphere, and the sky stretching far overhead upon all sides.

LEIGH HUNT (1784-1859)

Deep in the soul, below pain, below all the distraction of life, is a silence vast and grand – an infinite ocean of calm, which nothing can disturb; Nature's own exceeding peace, which 'passes understanding' That which we seek with passionate longing, here and there, upward and outward; we find at last within ourselves.

C.M.C. QUOTED BY R.M. BUCKE

*T*here is no quiet place in the white man's cities, no place to hear the leaves of spring or the rustle of insect's wings.... The Indians prefer the soft sound of the wind darting over the face of the pond, the smell of the wind itself cleansed by the midday rain, or scented with pinion pine.

CHIEF SEATTLE

Life just is. You have
to *flow* with it. Give
yourself to the moment.
Let it happen.

GOVERNOR JERRY BROWN

Arranging a bowl of

flowers in the morning

can give a sense of

quiet in a crowded day

– like writing a poem,

or saying a prayer.

ANNE MORROW LINDBERGH

Here will we sit
and let the
sounds of music creep in
our ears:
soft stillness and the
night become the
touches of sweet
harmony.

WILLIAM SHAKESPEARE
(1564-1616)

THE QUIETER YOU
BECOME, THE MORE
YOU CAN HEAR.

BABA RAM DASS

If we are not happy, if we are not peaceful, we cannot share peace and happiness with others, even those we love, those who live under the same roof. If we are peaceful, if we are happy, we can smile and blossom like a flower, and everyone in our family, our entire society, will benefit from our peace.

THICH NHAT HANH

*W*hen I set myself sometimes to consider the divers agitations of men, and the

*troubles and
dangers to which
they expose
themselves,.... I
see that all their
misfortunes come
from one thing
only, that they
know not how to
dwell in peace, in
a room.*

BLAISE PASCAL
(1623–1662)

Over

all the mountaintops

Is peace.

In all treetops

You perceive

Scarcely a breath.

The little birds in the forest

Are silent.

Wait then; soon

You, too, will have peace.

JOHANN WOLFGANG VON GOETHE
(1749-1832)

> *IF ONLY I MAY GROW: FIRMER, SIMPLER – QUIETER, WARMER.*

DAG HAMMARSKJÖLD

I lay in a meadow until the unwrinkled serenity entered into my bones, and made me into one with the browsing kine, the still greenery, the drifting clouds, and the swooping birds.

ALICE JAMES

I expand and live in the warm day like corn and melons.

RALPH WALDO EMERSON
(1803-1882)

Peace is not something you wish for; it's something you make, something you do, something you are, and something you give away!

ROBERT FULGHUM

*Serenity is active. It is a
gentle and firm
participation with trust.
Serenity is the relaxation
of our cells into who we
are and a quiet
celebration of that
relaxation.*

ANNE WILSON SCHAEF

*Peace is not a passive but
an active condition, not
a negation but an
affirmation. It is a
gesture as strong as war.*

MARY ROBERTS RINEHART

Come away from the din. Come away to the quiet fields, over which the great sky stretches, and where, between us and the stars, there

*lies but silence; and
there, in the
stillness let us listen to
the voice that is
speaking within us.*

JEROME K. JEROME (1859-1927).

May peace and peace
and peace be everywhere.

THE UPANISHADS (c. 900-600 BC)

The quiet mind
is richer than a
crown.
... Such sweet
content, such
minds, such
sleep, such bliss
Beggars enjoy
when princes oft
do miss.

ROBERT GREENE
(1558–1592)

My greatest wealth is the deep stillness in which I strive and grow and win what the world cannot take from me with fire or sword.

JOHANN WOLFGANG VON GOETHE
(1749-1832)

The poor long for riches and the rich for heaven, but the wise long for a state of tranquillity.

SWAMI RAMA

*U*ltimately we have just
one moral duty: to reclaim
large areas of peace in
ourselves, more and more
peace, and to reflect it
toward others. And the
more peace there is in us,
the more peace there will be
in our troubled world.

ETTY HILLESUM

PEACE IS INEVITABLE TO THOSE WHO OFFER PEACE.

FROM "A COURSE IN MIRACLES"

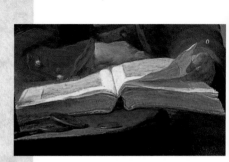

*The strong, calm man
is always loved and
revered. He is like a
shade-giving tree in a
thirsty land, or a
sheltering rock in a
storm.*

JAMES ALLEN (1864-1912)

FROM SERENITY COMES GENTLENESS, COMES LASTING STRENGTH.

PAM BROWN, b.1928

To a mind that is still the whole universe surrenders.

CHUANG TZU

Too many people, too many demands, too much to do; competent, busy, hurrying people – It just isn't living at all.

ANNE MORROW LINDBERGH

Life is eating us up. We shall be fables presently. Keep cool: it will be all one a hundred years hence.

RALPH WALDO EMERSON
(1803-1882)

*AND SO, WHILE
OTHERS MISERABLY
PLEDGE THEMSELVES
TO THE INSATIABLE
PURSUIT OF AMBITION*

AND BRIEF POWER,
I WILL BE STRETCHED
OUT IN THE SHADE,
SINGING.

FRAY LUIS DE LEÓN (c.1527–1591)

What life can compare to this? Sitting quietly by the window, I watch the leaves fall and the flowers bloom, as the seasons come and go.

HSUEH-TOU (950–1052)

Before me peaceful
Behind me peaceful
Under me peaceful
Over me peaceful
Around me peaceful

NAVAJO PRAYER

Acknowledgements: The publishers are grateful for permission to reproduce copyright material. Whilst every reasonable effort has been made to trace copyright holders, the publishers would be pleased to hear from any not here acknowledged. THICH NHAT HANH: From *Being Peace* (1987) by Thich Nhat Hanh with permission from Parallax Press, Berkeley, California. ETTY HILLESUM: From *An Interrupted Life – The Diaries of Etty Hillesum 1941-1943*. ANNE MORROW LINDBERGH: From *Bring Me A Unicorn*, published by Harcourt Brace Jovanovich. 1971, 1972 by Anne Morrow Lindbergh. J. DONALD WALTERS: From *"There's Joy in the Heavens"*, published by Crystal Clarity Publishers.

Picture credits: Exley Publications would like to thank the following organizations and individuals for permission to reproduce their pictures. Whilst every reasonable effort has been made to trace the copyright holders, the publishers would be pleased to hear from any not here acknowledged. Archiv für Kunst (AKG), Artworks (AW), Bridgeman Art Library (BAL), Fine Art Photographic Library (FAP), Giraudon (GIR), Index (IND), SuperStock (SS). Cover and title page: Claude Monet, *Waterlillies;* pages 6/7: Valentin Alexandrovitch Serov, *Pond in Thicket*, AKG; pages 8/9: © 1998 Walter Farmer, *Through a Window*, BAL; page 10: Norbert Goeneutte, *Doctor Paul Gachet*, GIR; page 12: Matias Morales, *Columbian Woman on a Divan*, SS; page 14: Gamaliel Subang, *Dining Table*; page 16: © 1998 Florence Eden, *The Little Weaver*, SS:

page 19: Aleksandr Andreevic Ivanov, *Water and Stones*, SS; page 21: Edouard Dubufe, *Portrait of Juliette Dubufe*, GIR; page 23: Eugene Boudin, *Trouville: The Pier*, GIR; pages 24/25: Pierre Auguste Renoir, *Summer Landscape*, BAL; page 26: Karoly Ferenczy, *Bird Song*, BAL; page 29: © 1998 Harold Speed, *The Garden Path*, SS; page 30: James Jacques Joseph Tissot, *Reverie: Mrs Newton Reclining in a Chair*, BAL; page 33: Berga I. Boix, *Countryside*, IND; pages 34/35: Elliot Clark, *Cold Spring Harbor*; page 37: Jean Hippolyle Flandrin, *Nude Young Man At The Seaside*, GIR; page 39: © 1998 Gyokudo Kawai, *Summer Shower*, BAL; pages 40/41: Timothy Easton, *Morning Break*, BAL; page 43: © 1998 Karen Armitage, *Agapanthus Molucela Arrangement in a Glass Vase*, BAL; page 44: John Atkinson Grimshaw, *Moonlight on the Lake, Roundhay Park*, FAP; page 47: *Home Sweet Home*; page 48: 1998 Juan Lascano, *Baskets of Bread*, SS; page 50: Paul Cezanne, *The Bridge At Maincy*, GIR/BAL; page 52/53: Adelsteen Normann, *Reflections in a Norwegian Fjord*, FAP; page 55: © 1998 Charles Neal, *River Nene*, SS; page 56: © 1998 Dame Laura Knight, *Summertime, Cornwall*, BAL; pages 58/59: John Ruskin, *Stormy Sunset*, BAL; pages 60/61: John Hollis Kaufmann, *Sea Change*, SS; page 62: © 1998 Rose Mary Barton, *The Haycart Approaches*, BAL; page 65: © 1998 Joel Spector, AW; page 66: J.S. Chardin, *Portrait of Jacques Aved*, GIR; page 68: Private Collection; pages 70/71: Vincent Van Gogh, *Garden of Daubigny*; page 73: © 1998 Alberto Pisa, *Holmwood, Surrey*, BAL; pages 74/75: Claude Monet, *Waterlillies*.